M. Hershberger

Rm. 30

No Lexile Found
2003

A DAY IN THE LIFE OF A
Fashion Designer

by Ann Hodgman
Photography by Gayle Jann

Troll Associates

Library of Congress Cataloging in Publication Data

Hodgman, Ann.
   A day in the life of a fashion designer.

   Summary: Follows a New York City fashion designer
through her day as she draws sketches, consults with pattern makers, meets with buyers from various stores, and
teaches at a design school.
   1. Steffe, Cynthia—Juvenile literature.   2. Costume
designers—United States—Biography—Juvenile literature.
3. Costume design—Vocational guidance—Juvenile
literature.   [1. Costume designers.   2. Steffe, Cynthia.
3. Costume design.   4. Occupations]   I. Jann, Gayle, ill.
II. Title.
TT505.S74H63   1988   746.9'2'0924   87-13394
ISBN 0-8167-1119-4 (lib. bdg.)
ISBN 0-8167-1120-8 (pbk.)

10   9   8   7   6   5   4   3   2   1

The author and publisher wish to thank Cynthia Steffe, Juo Yu, the staff of
Spitalnick Associates, and Kate Wiest for their assistance and cooperation.

Cynthia Steffe is a fashion designer in New York City. Her job is a demanding one, and she always tries to be at the office early. This gives her a chance to work on one of her sketches without interruptions. Drawing a sketch is the first step in creating a fashion design.

The fabric Cynthia wants to use for a new dress has been draped on a mannequin. Cynthia studied it carefully before she began sketching. She must always work with the fabric first in order to sketch the design most suited to it. A style designed for silk, for example, is very different from one designed for cotton.

When she has finished a sketch, Cynthia brings it
to one of her two pattern makers. He will study it
and make a pattern for a sample of the design.
New designs are always made in muslin, a plain
white cloth, before more expensive fabric is used.
This keeps costs down and allows Cynthia to make
changes as often as she needs to.

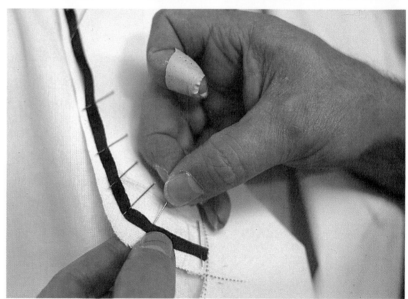

The muslin jacket hanging on the mannequin needs a few alterations. Cynthia and the pattern maker use strips of black cotton twill tape to mark the places where the changes will be made. In this case, the jacket's lapel needs to be narrower.

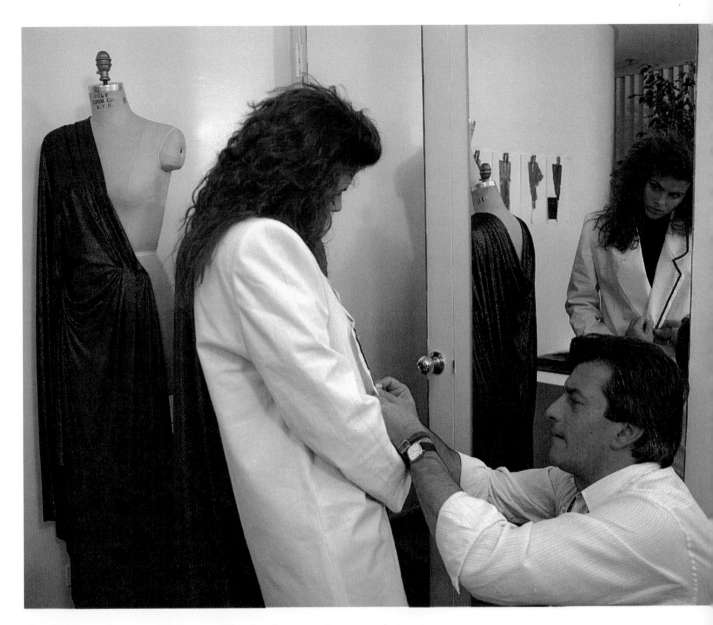

Cynthia tries on the muslin jacket so her assistant can pin it more easily. At this stage, she or one of her assistants will model the garments. Professional models will not be used until the jacket has been made in the real fabric.

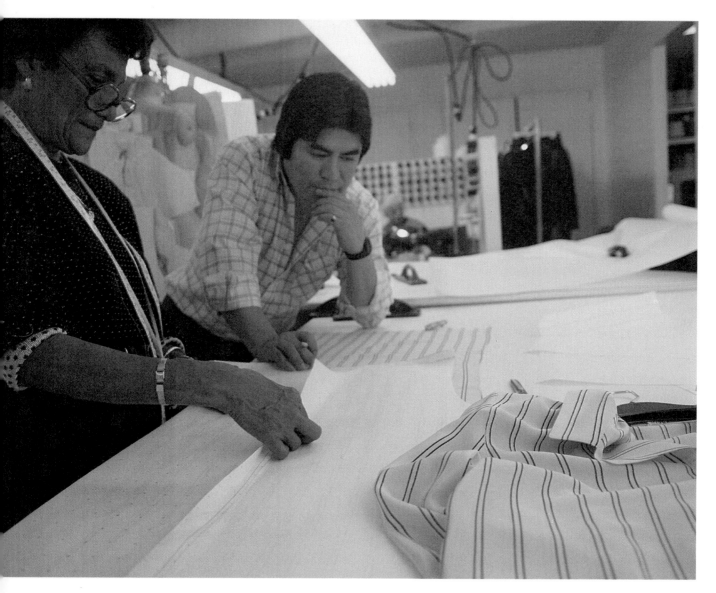

In the design room, samples are cut out in a fabric similar to the one that will be used in the finished garments. This fabric will be tested to see how it "reacts" to being cut, sewn, and worn. Once final changes have been made in the design, the garment will be put together in the real fabric.

All original designs are sewn into garments in the production room. Most of the sewing is done on machines, but some of the more delicate work must be done by hand. Each kind of thread is carefully chosen for thickness, strength, and color. Buttons, snaps, and zippers are added where they are called for.

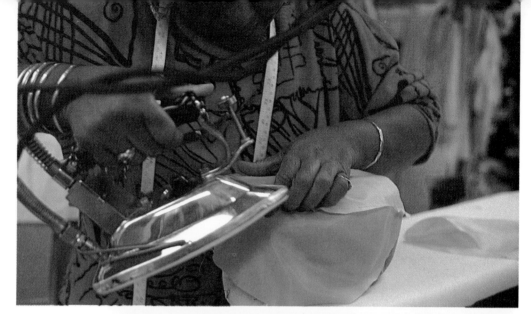

As it is being sewn, each garment must be pressed frequently. Once the garment has been completed and approved, the original pattern will be sent to the production department. It will take about four months from the time the fabric is ordered to the time the first mass-produced garment is finished.

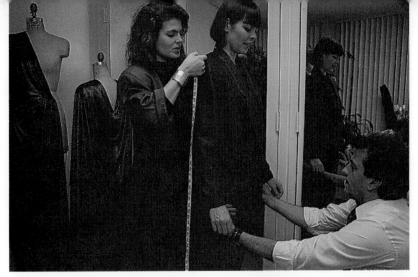

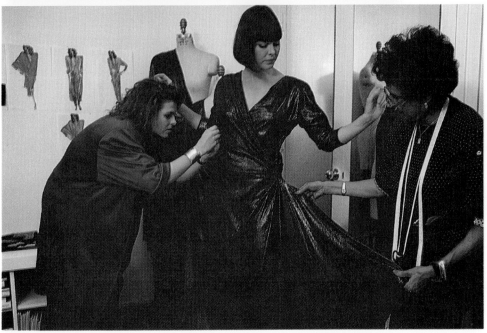

Back in Cynthia's office, a professional model is used to check the fit of each finished piece of clothing. The model's proportions are perfect for Cynthia's designs—an exact size eight. Cynthia's clothes range from size four through size fourteen. Since size eight is in the middle of the range, most sample garments are eights.

A skilled artist studies one of Cynthia's fabric designs, then reproduces the design with a paintbrush. Later, Cynthia will carefully examine the painting. The colors and pattern must be duplicated exactly.

Cynthia also checks the painting of the fabric design to make sure it will work with different kinds of fabric. When the painting is finished and approved, it will be taken to Italy. There a special screen will be made and the design will be printed in silk.

Fabric salespeople often come to Cynthia's office—sometimes from as far away as Italy—to show her their fabric "lines," or collections. Fabric companies create several lines each year, usually one for each season. Like all fashion designers, Cynthia designs different clothes for summer, fall, winter, and spring.

While Cynthia meets with one salesman, her assistant is busy with another one from New York. Cynthia and Kate are choosing fabrics for two seasons ahead. They must order their fabric far in advance of the time they will need it. Sample cloth, or yardage, may take three months to arrive.

Often Cynthia has business lunches away from her office. Today, to save time, she and Kate are having a "working lunch" in the office so they can compare fabric samples. A dark-red cashmere jacquard may be just the thing for the fall collection.

16

Joanne is a weaving technician in Cynthia's office. Using graph paper, she sketches a new pattern for a computerized hand loom. When Cynthia has approved the pattern, Joanne will program it into the loom's computer. She uses a magnifying glass to count the number of threads in fabric samples.

To prepare yarn for the loom, thread is wound on a special board. Joanne's hands race back and forth as she winds the thread. Then she loops the yarn into a braid to keep it from tangling as she puts it on the loom.

Joanne programs the loom before weaving the pattern she has created. Samples of different patterns are pinned up so she can study them from a distance. Cynthia will choose colors for the final designs. Then the designs will be taken to a mill in Italy, and sample fabric will be made from them.

A magazine's fashion editor has come to interview Cynthia about her collection for next season. Each issue of a fashion magazine must be planned several months before the magazine is actually sold. The editor will feature outfits from as many designers as possible.

In her showroom, Cynthia meets with buyers
from various stores. Buyers select and purchase
the clothes their stores will offer each season.
They, too, must work several months in advance.
Cynthia often helps them prepare their catalogs
and advertisements. She also offers advice on
which outfits to display in their store windows.

In the early afternoon, Cynthia leaves her office to visit Parsons School of Design. She studied fashion here and was named "Student Designer of the Year" as a senior. Now she teaches at Parsons, helping other seniors with their final projects. Many top designers teach at Parsons.

For one class, students have been asked to design three separate outfits—one for spring, one for fall, and one for evening wear. Cynthia will advise them on the fall designs. First she reviews the students' sketches, choosing the one with the best "look." Where necessary, she makes suggestions for revising the sketches.

Many students' sketches are displayed for Cynthia's reviews and comments. Most fashion drawings show very tall, thin models—much taller and thinner than most real people. This sets off the clothes better than a more realistic drawing would.

Like Cynthia's designs, the students' designs are first made in muslin. A student's sketch of a new jacket is taped to a mannequin wearing the same garment. Cynthia studies the sketch when she evaluates the jacket. Next, professional models are brought in. Cynthia checks to make sure the tailoring is headed in the right direction.

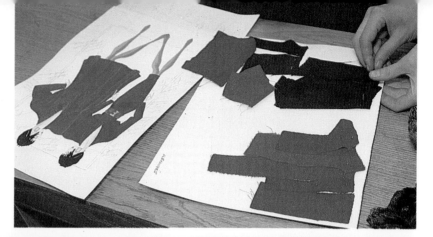

After they have made their designs in muslin, the students are ready to choose real fabrics. They research fabrics on their own, then bring in samples to discuss with Cynthia. Color is very important in choosing a fabric, of course. But its texture, weight, and the way it can be shaped in garments must also be considered.

Cynthia's designs are carried in major New York department stores. After leaving Parsons, she makes a surprise visit to one store to check on her clothes. She wants to be sure they are pressed, hung, and arranged properly. If they are not, Cynthia will ask for changes.

After leaving the store, Cynthia must prepare for a "presskit shoot," or photography session. She makes a last-minute alteration to a model's skirt so the hem will look right in the presskit photo. Designers and manufacturers use presskits to publicize each new collection. Kits are sent to newspapers and magazines all over the country.

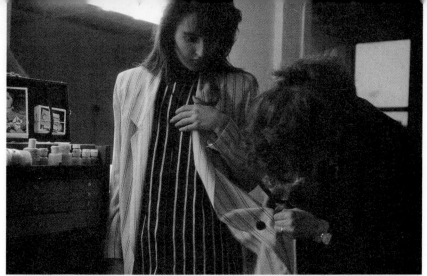

Each presskit contains a short biography of Cynthia and several photos of her latest fashions. Kate helps to get a model ready for a shot of a new jacket. The way the model's hair is arranged will make a big difference to the jacket's appearance. So Kate must check her hairstyle, too.

For this shoot, each model is posed in front of a neutral gray backdrop. This will show the cut of the clothes better, and make the fabrics stand out more. A brightly colored backdrop might take away attention from the clothes.

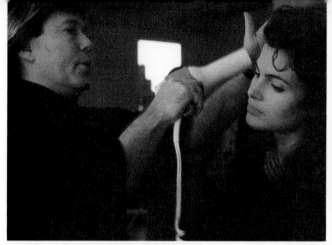

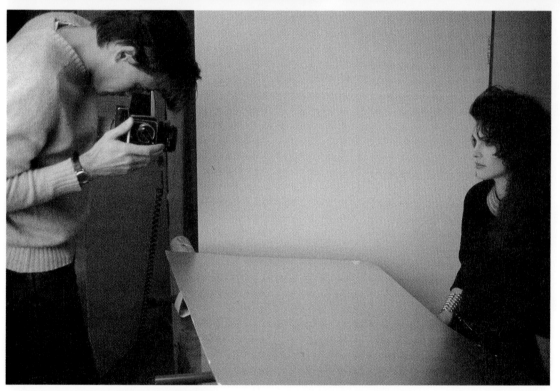

Now it is Cynthia's turn to have her picture taken for the presskit. A former model herself, she is used to being in front of a camera. The stylist checks her hair and makeup. Then the photographer takes a Polaroid shot to make sure the light is right for the portrait.

Cynthia's long day is not over yet. Tonight she will fly to Italy to work on fabrics and order sample yardage for her next collection. She takes a limousine to the heliport, where a helicopter is waiting to take her to the airport. Cynthia's job isn't always this glamorous, but she enjoys everything about being a fashion designer.